ST. NORBERT

AND

HIS ORDER

By a Norbertine Father

𝕸𝖊𝖉𝖎𝖆𝖙𝖗𝖎𝖝 𝕻𝖗𝖊𝖘𝖘

MMXV

ISBN: 0692531068

© Mediatrix Press 2015

Originally published by:
St. Norbert's College Press
11 July 1955

Cover: *The Consecration of St. Norbert*
Abraham van Diepenbeeck

Nihil obstat: D. H. Hockers, O. Praem.
Censor deputatus

Imprimi potest:
✠ S Killeen, O. Praem.
Abbot of St. Norbert Abbey
West De Pere, Wisconsin

Imprimatur:
✠ Stanislaus Bona, D.D.
Bishop of Green Bay
June 11, 1955

TABLE OF CONTENTS

In memory of
Dr. John and Penny Thornbrugh.

S. NORBERTVS

Teutonicus, Xantis illustri genere
ortus, in Præmonstrato candidum
Ordinem sub regula S. Augustini instituit
anno 1120. probante Honorio II. Moritur
Archiepiscopus Magdeburgensis a: 1134.

Cornelius Galle   T. Galle excud.
sculpsit.   cum privilegio

INTRODUCTION

THE Order of St. Norbert occupies an important place in the history of religious orders. It establishes a noteworthy link between the ancient and modern forms of the religious life with all its varied and beneficent activity for the human race.

Norbert was a pioneer; and his foundation is a happy and successful mixture of the spiritual elements which constitute the perfect priestly and religious life.

The Order of Prémontré represents in medieval and modern society, a form of sacerdotal life which, during many centuries, was deemed the ideal of the clerical profession, the guarantee of its interior sanctity and its exterior reputation. It unites in itself all that stamps the life of the active priest as a worthy imitation and continuation of the life of Christ's own disciples, protecting them, by the common life, against an ever threatening spirit of worldliness and at the same time raising the sacerdotal labor for the salvation of souls to the highest pitch of intensity, by the law of love and the example of the Savior who sent out his apostles two by two. The common life, moreover, enables the clergy to perform the liturgical functions of the Church with greater magnificence and decorum, which thus deepen the spirituality of the people and refresh their entire supernatural life.

The comparison of the Catholic Church with an ancient majestic cathedral is obvious. Not only because of her eternal beauty as the Bride of Christ, richly and artistically decorated, nor on account of her solidity, braving the storms and the elements of ages, founded on the imperishable rock by the divine Artist, who is himself the chief cornerstone; but also because the Church, like an ancient cathedral, preserving the monuments of the changing art of many past and distant generations, protects its foundations and institutes which rose as spiritual masterpieces under the steady influence of the Holy Spirit, who renews men and their times for the perpetual enrichment of the Christian life. The observance of the evangelical counsels and the continuation of the apostolic or priestly life and labors have ornamented the Church of God with magnificent masterpieces and monuments. Sometimes both are united in the same institute, at other periods they are strictly separated, each supporting itself. Both, however, with all their diversity of development, preserved their essential interior elements which characterize them as divine institutions, united always with the Church itself, whose mysterious life, on account of this dualism, seems sometimes enigmatic, but remains ever grand, noble, and admirable in the manifold manifestations of its activity.

In the early ages of Christianity, monastic life and priestly vocation stand far apart, though both rest on the same divine foundation.

Monasticism is nothing else but the socialization of asceticism. It is the common exercise of the evangelical counsels and whatever is necessary or useful for the safer and securer observance of the spiritual life.

The priesthood, on the other hand, is the continuation of the apostolic life, of the administration of the Sacraments instituted by Christ, the preaching of the Gospel, and the distribution of grace among the Christian people, by virtue of ordination and mission by the Church of God.

In the early centuries of the Christian era monasticism was mainly constituted by the laity, though the priestly class might form part of it. The clergy constituted the various degrees of the ecclesiastical hierarchy and had an official character through ordination and jurisdiction.

In the course of time, both institutes or orders approached each other. Pope Gregory the Great strictly upheld the lay character of monasticism by legislating that no priest could be abbot of a community. However, he knew no better missionaries and apostles than the monks.

For a long time during the Middle Ages "*vita apostolica*" (to live after the manner of the Apostles) meant primarily, to live in community, which is identical with "canonical" or "religious life." Only later on "apostolic life" came to signify missionary activity either among the Christians or the pagans.

Introduction

In theory as well as in practice it is not difficult to understand the intermingling of monastic and clerical life, which is found frequently in the fourth century and which was almost the rule in Western Europe from the fifth to the tenth century. It has been praised by many popes, and recently by Pius X, as the ideal life of the clergy.

If monasticism is the social form of the devout and perfect Christian life, it is evident that the true priest feels himself closely related to it, because he has preeminently a social vocation as the mediator between the people and God, and between God and the people. He is an *alter Christus*, another Christ. The entire reason of his existence and especially his highest function offering sacrifice — bears a social character. What was practically united in the life of Christ and His Apostles, i. e., the priesthood and religious life, would appear, from history, the safest and the most honorable form of living. Besides, the laity loved to see their priests live according to the evangelical counsels which they were to preach and promote among their flock.

In these facts and principles we discover the "canonizing" of the clergy. The "clericalizing" of the monks rests fundamentally on the same motives.

The elite of the monks, educated in the cloister, were promoted to various ecclesiastical dignities; and thus it becomes intelligible, how in the course of time, the monasteries became the training schools for the priesthood.

Montalembert has given us a striking list of names, from which it appears how, outside the Gallo-Roman cities, parochial life grew to a large extent out of monastic institutions. In these cities, or outside of them, the bishop lived with his clergy in community life, as we know from the history of St. Martin.

Up to the thirteenth century the care of souls was largely in the hands of regulars or seculars who lived in common. The majority of the churches, in some districts nearly all of them, were convent or collegiate churches, or at least affiliated with some religious order.

In the successive reforms of the clergy, one of the most insistent demands was the "*vita communis*" (the common life). Thus it was between 712 and 816, with the reforms inaugurated by Saint Chrodogang of Metz and continued till the Council of Aix-La-Chapelle. Again, under the pontificate of the indomitable Gregory VII, though his ordinances were provisionally destined only for the priests in the Roman provinces.

From the nature of the case, reforms frequently fail to be entirely successful and bring only a partial amelioration of misshapen conditions. Strict,—sometimes excessively rigorous—in abolishing the most scandalous abuses, the reformers permitted conditions which, though less dangerous, are, on account of their apparent insignificance, apt to frustrate largely the end and object of the reforms. They have, therefore, within themselves the germ of failure.

Thus in the reforming measures of St. Chrodogang the essence of the common life was infected by the neglect of introducing community of goods, or strict poverty. As long as private or personal property was permitted—contemporary and later historians agree in this—the regular or monastic life of the clergy was by anticipation condemned to die. This was the more certain because the Church itself was on its human side largely organized on a feudal basis. This private property became the foundation of hierarchical authority and spiritual service or the care of souls. The entire matter of ecclesiastical benefices—in spite of its many excellent qualities and advantages—rested on personal property. This brought about a degeneration of the clergy, many of whom became capitalistic or feudalistic proprietors.

The Order of St. Norbert originated in the twelfth century as a masterpiece of unequalled beauty. It arose in an age of transition. As the artistic monuments of the transition period between Roman and Gothic possess certain peculiar charms, a freshness of youth and growth, a variety of motion and development, so also with the Norbertine Order. And, as many an artist is more interested in a medieval building, showing a mixture of Roman and Gothic, than in a masterpiece of the purest Gothic, so does the attractive type of medieval clerical life, adapted to modern conditions, fascinate the mind of man and is to him a perpetual source of delight, "a thing of beauty" and "a joy forever." Though the plan of St. Norbert was not entirely original, still he may truly be called a pioneer, who united in one institute contemplation and action, social asceticism and the priesthood, under perfect obedience to the supreme Head of the Church. "*Ad omne opus bonum paratus,*" (Ready for every good work) was his motto. The Order thus adapted itself almost spontaneously to the changing forms and conditions of society. It is to this rather than to anything else that it owes the privilege of sharing in the characteristic attribute of the Church — viz. perpetuity. While, of the many medieval canonical institutes, only a few have remained, the order of St. Norbert was destined to preserve in this secularized age a remembrance of that harmonious priestly life in which Mary and Martha, prayer and work, contemplation and action, take turns in the unceasing worship of the Almighty.

The Norbertine life, therefore, is like that of the angels, who while seeing God face to face, devote themselves to the custody and care of souls.

Our times have their own demands. Urgent necessities claim almost the entire activity of the priest. Remarkable is the manifestation of God's Spirit in the life of Catholicism. With the social and public activity of the clergy coincides the revival of the liturgy; and no good canon or priest ever thinks of separating the Divine Office and the Sacrifice of the Mass from his daily labors.

* * *

The mutual interaction between sacerdotalism and monasticism is one of the most wonderful things in the history of the Catholic Church. Alternately repelling and attracting each other, they constantly exercise a mutual influence upon each other which is beneficial. When the one becomes secularized, the other spiritualizes or "clericalizes" itself. And though the official functions of the priesthood exercise occasionally a relaxing influence on monastic life, the intelligent and friendly relations between regulars and seculars, especially since the Council of Trent, have brought a complete change in the life and labors of the secular clergy.

* * *

Where Gregory VII failed almost entirely, Norbert succeeded wonderfully, — we may say, miraculously.

There is no more evident argument or more striking example of the tenaciousness of inveterate customs condemned by the Church, than the condition of affairs after the reforming ordinances of this titanic pope, who could bend the neck of emperors but was almost impotent against the clergy. The priests,—thus decreed Gregory,— should live, as in the times of the Fathers, canonically, i. e. according to a definite rule. Some willingly obeyed his orders, but many refused to do so and in this we find the origin of an anomaly: a secular canonical clergy or a regular (canon) without a rule.

The unbroken existence of this remarkable Order is greater honor than any human hymn of praise. In the history of this world, where man spends his days in constructive and destructive work, over eight centuries of uninterrupted existence and beneficent influence are an eloquent proof of superhuman worth.

If you wish to appreciate a work of art according to its value and show its beauty to advantage, you must give it an historical setting.

Who knows what may in the coming centuries be the glories and triumphs of this ancient Order, twice the age of the oldest Protestant sect.

Many forms of religious life will adorn the fair brow of the Catholic Church in future ages. As long as the Church will exist, viz: until the end of time, she will be the prolific mother of spiritual and religious institutions adapted to the changing needs of the times.

If the past is a prophecy of the future, the Order of St. Norbert will continue to exist and flourish in the midst of the elemental evolutions and revolutions of the world, recording its ancient glories and developing its strength, thus giving testimony by its inherent excellence, of a beautiful embodiment of zeal and sanctity.

PART ONE
SAINT NORBERT

Chapter I
His Early Life

SAINT Norbert was born at Xanten, Germany, towards the close of the eleventh century, (1080). His father, a member of the highest nobility of the land, was count of Gennep, while his mother was related to the royal house of France.

Being of noble descent, Norbert could look forward to a brilliant career. He received his early education from his parents, who were God-fearing people, and, in course of time he entered the service of God by receiving the dignity of subdeacon, and became a canon of the collegiate church of Xanten. This, however, was rather human foresight than the result of a divine vocation. It was the custom in those days, for the youngest son of a nobleman to embrace the clerical state in order to obtain, in the course of time, the highest ecclesiastical dignities, and reap the benefits of the benefices attached thereto.

Part One: St. Norbert

The question of vocation was often entirely overlooked.

The young canon led a worldly life, ill-befitting his state. He soon abandoned his canonical office to become a member of the episcopal court at Cologne and later, of the imperial household. Henry V, the reigning monarch, loved the young nobleman, who by his courtly manners, extensive learning, and knightly appearance, soon endeared himself to all with whom he came in touch.

Norbert, likewise, entertained a strong affection towards his royal master. He assisted him by word and deed to attain the realization of his imperial plans, even so far as to take his side against the Pope, and to accompany him on his journey to Rome. But when Norbert was there, and the emperor, having little respect for honor or honesty, even made Pope Pascal II a prisoner, he grew disgusted with him. He realized his mistake, and left the court, in spite of kind words, promises, and costly presents. This was his first step on the road to God. Mundane majesty and worldly pleasures, however, still captivated the heart of the young nobleman, and there was nothing about him which would mark him as the future founder of a great religious Order. But strange things were to happen shortly.

Chapter II
The Storm

During the summer of the year 1115, Norbert, bent upon gaiety and pleasure, was making his way on a fiery steed to Freden, his servant riding by his side. Suddenly, dark clouds covered the sky. A violent wind arose, and vivid flashes of lightning and rumbling peals of thunder followed one another in rapid succession. Norbert, although trembling with a strange fear, insisted nevertheless on continuing the journey. His servant, not so courageous, stopped his terrified charger and exclaimed: "Sir Norbert, whither art thou going? Come back! The hand of God is against thee!"

Hardly had he spoken these words when a flash, more vivid and dazzling than the rest, struck Norbert's horse and threw the dazed rider to the ground. For a time, he lay there like one dead. When he regained

consciousness, the last words of his page —
"The hand of God is against thee" — were
still ringing in his ears. They were to him
like a message from heaven. Realizing the
great danger he had just escaped, Norbert
cried out with Saint Paul, "Lord, what wilt
Thou that I should do?" And immediately, a
voice from heaven sounded in his ear,
saying, "Turn away from evil, and do good.
Seek after peace and pursue it!"

Norbert rose. His love of pleasure had
vanished. It was the turning point of his
life. Having returned to Xanten, he learned
to love solitude, and began to meditate on
the fundamental truths of Christianity. For
three years he practiced severe penance;
fasting, vigils, and prayer constituted his
daily occupation. And when the time came
for ordinations, he asked to be raised to the
dignity of deacon and priest.

Chapter III
Ardent Faith of St. Norbert

AFTER his ordination, Norbert gave
evidence of wonderful virtues. Once
when he was offering up the Holy

Sacrifice of the Mass in a grotto, at the moment of Consecration a large ugly-looking spider fell into the Precious Blood. In those days, spiders were generally considered poisonous, as the old English name "attercop," (poison-cup), still indicates. The Saint was well aware that the rubrics allowed him to remove the insect and burn it, but so great was his reverence for the Precious Blood, that at the Communion of the Mass, ready to die at the altar, he drank the Sacred Blood containing the presumably poisonous spider. To die out of reverence for the Blessed Sacrament seemed to him the highest happiness. But God rewarded the lively faith of his servant. He sneezed and was thus relieved of the nauseating creature, through his nose.

No wonder that the grateful priest was, later on, so willing to defend the Eucharist against the heresies of Tankelin. Not without reason, therefore, did his contemporaries praise his faith, saying, "In Bernard shines charity; in Milo, humility; in Norbert, faith."

Chapter IV
His Zeal For Souls

THE young priest made rapid progress on the path of virtue and perfection. He had renounced his canonical benefices, and had given the emoluments to the Bishop of Cologne. Now he sold his own possessions, and gave the proceeds to the poor and needy. A few pieces of silver, the sacred vestments, and a mule were all that he retained. Accompanied by two servants, who refused to abandon their master, he left his native town, barefooted and bareheaded. From now on he would, as a tireless missionary, travel through Europe, preaching the Word of God.

To avoid all opposition on the part of the clergy, he paid a visit to Pope Gelasius II, at St. Gilles, in France. He both asked and obtained permission to preach everywhere as an apostolic missionary. He announced the Word of God in eloquent language, at Orleans, Valenciennes, Cambray, and in the greater part of the provinces of Hainault and Brabant.

St. Norbert and His Order

His name was on the lips of all. Whenever it was known that he was in the neighborhood, people flocked from all sides to hear him. The bells of the churches would ring out joyfully, inviting all the faithful to come to hear the great and saintly preacher.

With what intense devotion they knelt around the altar when he offered the great Sacrifice of the Mass! With what rapt attention did they listen to his glowing words! Numberless were the converts, snatched from the clutches of sin and heresy by the mighty words of the zealous and eloquent missionary. He was hailed as an angel of peace and charity, sent from heaven for the salvation of the people, who vied with each other to have him as their guest. Norbert dreaded all pomp and luxury, and even the poorest could provide for him all he wished. He loved to eat from the floor. Bread, vegetables, salt, and water were more than sufficient for him.

Thus, by his example he taught the people love of virtue, and spurred them on to lead better and holier lives. And it seemed that God had given him special graces to reconcile inveterate enemies and to convert obstinate sinners.

Chapter V
Callistus II and Norbert

Pope Gelasius died in the beginning of the year 1119, and Norbert was obliged to ask the new pontiff to confirm the apostolic letters granted by his predecessor. Accompanied by Blessed Hugh of Fosse, his first and most faithful disciple, he went to the Council of Rheims, but the great concourse of priests and noblemen prevented his access to the Holy Father. Disappointed, but not disheartened, Norbert left the city to reflect in solitude on his future mission. He had been praying for a long time by the roadside, when a brilliant cortege passed by. It was Bartholomew, the bishop of Laon, a blood relation of Callistus II.

Moved by the sight of the Saint, whose features mirrored the noble virtues and graces he possessed, the bishop approached him and tenderly asked him the cause of his sadness. Norbert's answer was simple and humble. Hugh, however, related to the bishop the story of Norbert's noble descent, his voluntary poverty and apostolic zeal. Bartholomew gave ardent thanks to God for this happy meeting, and promised Norbert an audience with the Sovereign Pontiff.

Callistus II listened benevolently to the request of the saintly missionary, and granted him extensive faculties, expressing his hope of a more lengthy interview in the episcopal palace at Laon.

At this second conference with the pope, ways and means were thought out to hasten the realization of Norbert's plans.

"Your eloquent and powerful preaching will do a great deal of good throughout Europe," the Holy Father remarked, "but it were better to establish yourself in some convent and gather disciples around you to train them to continue your work after your death."

This suggestion was heartily supported by the bishop of Laon, who promised to look for a suitable place in his own diocese. Nor did Norbert disdain these wise counsels. He gratefully accepted the bishop's proposal, and thanked the Holy Father for his kindness and encouragement.

Chapter VI
The Chapel of St. John The Baptist

BARTHOLOMEW suggested to his saintly friend numerous wealthy abbeys encircled by beautiful landscapes, as possible locations for his work; but Norbert rejected all these and sought only for a humble and lowly place.

One day, in their travels, the bishop and Norbert passed a narrow valley, covered with swamp and forest land. But no sooner did Norbert's eyes fall on the place than he fervently thanked God, and exclaimed: "Here shall I live all the days of my life; this spot God has prepared for me for all eternity."

At the entrance to the valley stood a little chapel, which had, some years past, been built by the monks of St. Benedict and was dedicated to St. John the Baptist. Yet, the little building had long since been abandoned, and was almost completely in ruins. Norbert asked permission of his companion, the bishop, to spend the night there in prayer. The bishop gave assent and withdrew.

Thus, early on the bright morning of the following day, the bishop returned and stood waiting at the door of the chapel. With a serene and joyful countenance, Norbert met him. Wonderful visions had he seen during the night, for God had revealed to his eyes the secrets of the future, and shown him a numerous group of pilgrims, making their way through the valley, bearing crosses, candles and censers in their hands, and singing songs of praise to the Most High, as they proceeded on their way. Above all, during the night the heavens were opened to Norbert and he saw a vision of the Blessed Virgin, with angels all about. She told him that his prayers were heard, and pointed out to him where he would build the first house of the Order. Lastly, she showed to him the white habit and said: "Receive my son the white habit." It is from this vision that Norbert and his order thereafter have worn this color.

"I am sure, my Father," he said to the bishop, "that in this place, many brethren will work out their salvation. Here I must sing the praises of the Lord, together with faithful companions, whom God will send me."

Through the aid of the good prelate, the valley of Prémontré, (for such was its name) belonged to Norbert in a short time. Immediate preparations were made for the cultivation of the soil and the erection of a church and monastery. Disciples poured in from all sides, and on Christmas night, 1121, they pronounced their first vows.

Chapter VII
The Apostle Of The Blessed Sacrament

IN some countries of Europe, especially Belgium, Holland, and France, a new heretical religion was being preached by a fanatic named Tankelin. In his insane pride, he claimed to be the equal of the Son of God. In him alone, he said, was truth to be found, for the Holy Spirit had endowed him with extraordinary divine gifts. He denied the power of orders as well the authority of priests, bishops and even the Pope, while declaring that "the Church is I and my followers." Many sensual and ignorant people were seduced by this false and licentious blackguard who called vice virtue, and changed the truth of God into a lie.

Tankelin and his followers destroyed images and also preached against all moral restraint, adopting Manichean doctrines. Yet, the main object of his vicious attack was the holiest institution of Christendom, the Sacrament of the Altar. He blasphemed the Mass, and his diabolical example and execrable teaching led the people to commit the most revolting sacrileges. Tankelin had died, but his followers perpetuated this lamentable heresy. Antwerp was the chief stronghold of this heresy, and nearly the entire population had lost the Faith. Thus, this flourishing commercial city was the center from which was diffused throughout the neighboring places, the deadly miasma of "Tankelinism."

Part One: St. Norbert

In vain did the bishop of Cambray, in whose diocese Antwerp was located, labor to lead the stray sheep back to the fold, until at last he had recourse to Norbert. The Saint with some of his disciples, through their untiring zeal and kind and persuasive words, at last succeeded in winning back to the true fold a number of lost sheep, who had been led astray by Tankelin. "Brethren," he said, "I am aware that ignorance of the truth rather than love of error is the cause of your renouncing the true religion. Had the truth been announced to you, I know you would have followed it with as great eagerness as you have followed after error. You suffered yourselves to be misled, and now I hope you will allow yourselves to be saved by us." Thus, in his addresses to the people, he combined the gentleness of persuasion with the force of conclusive argument couched in simple language. No censure or reproach, no polemics or invectives, but working truth in charity, following the "more excellent way" of the great Apostle of the Gentiles. Well did he realize that "the Church cannot be built upon the ruins of charity." Soon all traces of

Tankelin's scandalous and impious teaching had disappeared. The grateful bishop, to recompense Norbert and his disciples, gave them the church which was the beginning of the famous abbey of St. Michael. From hence have sprung forth the monasteries of Middelburg, Averbode, and Tongerloo.

Chapter VIII
The Humility Of St. Norbert

AT the completion of this great missionary work, Norbert went to Rome in 1125, to ask of Pope Honorious II, the approbation of his Order. During his absence, Prior Hugh of Fosse acted as administrator and superior of the abbey. He was a strict, but loving master, excelling in charity towards the poor. During the famine of 1125, he fed more than five hundred needy people daily, from the goods of the abbey.

When Norbert returned, he rebuked Hugh for having so lavishly spent the goods of the community. But he soon regretted his sharp and hasty words. His tender heart reproached him for his severity, and so great was his humility, that he made an open confession of his fault. "Continue, my brethren," he said, "to feed and support the hungry, and pardon me my untimely rebuke and my lack of trust in the care and solicitude of Divine Providence."

Chapter IX
The Archbishop of Magdeburg

What a happy and peaceful life Norbert led with his brethren! "I have lived at court, and in the cloister," he often remarked, "but at court I was never happy; while in the monastery, I have never known unhappiness." He was soon to be removed from his blessed solitude. It was in the spring of the year 1126 that Norbert left his brethren and set out for the city of Spires.

When he arrived, an important meeting of bishops and nobles was being held, to discuss various important affairs pertaining to the welfare of the nation. One of the objects of the assembly was the appointment of a new archbishop to the primatial See of Germany, Magdeburg. The former primate, Rodger, had been dead for some time, but as yet no agreement had been reached as to his successor. Delegates had been sent to the imperial diet in order to hasten the appointment, but great difficulties arose, which, however, were overcome by the arrival of Norbert.

Many of those present at the assembly knew him personally. His knowledge, piety, and zeal for souls, were well known both to the clergy and to the laity. He was chosen archbishop in spite of his remonstrances, and the choice was readily confirmed by the emperor Lothaire, and by the papal delegate.

Chapter X
A Strange Beggar

ACCOMPANIED by members of the clergy and nobility, and various friends, Norbert set out from Spires to take possession of his newly-acquired see. His journey was a veritable triumphal march. Everywhere he was hailed and acclaimed as the primate of Germany, and the people knelt in the streets, as he passed by, to ask his blessing.

It was an edifying spectacle to the inhabitants of Magdeburg to see the humble Saint enter the city, walking barefoot, with no external pomp or ostentation whatever, looking more like a penitent or a beggar, than an archbishop. In the midst of princes and bishops, who acted as his escort, he seemed the least and lowliest of all. "What a holy shepherd of souls," they said: "how modest and how gentle!"

Having entered the cathedral church of the city, the procession continued on its way to the episcopal palace. The porter permitted all the members of the cortege to enter, but when Norbert came, last of all, he repulsed him angrily, saying, "Do you not see that you are out of place here?" The Saint, in no way offended, smiled, but those around him cried out, "Shame! He is our bishop!"

The poor servant was about to run away through fear of the consequences of his mistake, but Norbert stayed him, and said kindly, "You know me better, my good man, than those who have elevated me to this high dignity."

The news of this incident spread rapidly through the city. It confirmed the impressions of the people, who had been edified by his humble appearance, and made the new archbishop the firm friend of the poor and humble.

Chapter XI
The Courage Of Saint Norbert

THE triumphal march of Norbert, may fittingly be compared to Our Lord's entry into Jerusalem on Palm Sunday, for the joy of his adherents was soon turned to sorrow.

On account of the long vacancy in the episcopal see, many crying abuses had crept into the diocese of Magdeburg. Worldliness had invaded the sanctuary, and secular princes had usurped to themselves the prerogatives of the priesthood. Against both these evils Norbert waged bitter and relentless warfare.

First, he demanded the return of all property stolen from the archdiocese by secular princes, who made no efforts to hide their dislike for the new primate. They declared: "Why should we suffer a stranger, poor and unarmed, who made his entrance amongst us without anything but his donkey, to give us such haughty and peremptory orders! If he really is a saint, as his friends are pleased to tell us, why does he not then live on the revenue that was sufficient for his predecessor?

Norbert, however, remained firm in his resolve to recover whatever belonged to the church entrusted to him. He made use of his last recourse, excommunication, which in those days did not only affect one in matters of religion, but carried with it even civil penalties. The secular princes, excommunicated by St. Norbert, finally yielded and made reparation for their sacrileges.

St. Norbert's efforts to reform the clergy met with equally strong opposition. The canons of the cathedral openly rebelled against their bishop, and endeavored to frustrate all his divinely inspired plans. The cathedral had been profaned by a revolting crime, and had to be reconsecrated. The archbishop decided to perform the ceremony during the night, but the canons rang the bells and told the people that Norbert intended to steal the holy relics and treasures and give them to the various churches of his Order. They well knew that nothing would infuriate the people more than the danger of losing their precious relics. An excited and turbulent mob surrounded the church, shouting: "Our relics are being stolen!"

Although these wild cries terrified Norbert's assistants, the Saint remained calm and fearless. He advanced towards the door with the intention of going out to pacify the surging mob, had not the other bishops and priests prevented him. They persuaded him to accompany them to a place of safety in the old tower of the fortress built by Otto I.

Wonderful contrast! In the streets wild shouts and mad cries from the infuriated mob were rending the air, a maddened crowd crying for the life of the archbishop, while within, high in the tower, solemn and grave voices chanted the praises of the

Most High, and recounted the heroic virtues of the great Apostle.

From this time on, matters steadily grew worse until Norbert was at last driven from the diocese. He found a place of refuge with the hospitable Augustinians in their monastery near Halle. In the meantime, the Saint prayed for the sins of his people, and like another Paul, offered himself for their salvation. The all-merciful God graciously heard his prayer, softened the hard-hearted members of Norbert's flock, and caused sincere repentance among both the people and the clergy of Magdeburg.

Chapter XII
A Defender of the Papacy

THE last six years of Norbert's life were full of tireless activity and marked by great undertakings. With all his strength, he labored for the conversion of the Slavic races, took an active interest in the affairs of his Order, founded many monasteries, and acted as chief counsellor of the emperor, in the government of the nation. Above all, however, he was strongly attached to the Father of Christendom, the Pope of Rome. This attachment and loyalty he proved by his defense of the rights of Innocent II against the schismatic Peter Leonis, who by armed force seized Saint Peter's and was proclaimed pope by his adherents, under the name of Anacletus II.

Norbert eloquently spoke and pleaded at imperial diets and ecclesiastical councils in favor of the lawful pope. He at last succeeded in persuading Lothaire to organize a campaign in Italy in order to dethrone the usurper.

His strongest support in all these struggles was Saint Bernard, the most eloquent man of the age. Together they untiringly fought to protect the Church against its manifold enemies. At last, Innocent II, under imperial escort, entered the Eternal City in triumph, and once again ascended the papal throne, welcomed and lauded by all.

Chapter XIII
The Death of St. Norbert

The hardships incurred on his journey, the excessive heat of the summer, and his austere life, aggravated, to an alarming degree, the infirmities of the Saint. From that time on, he was almost continually subject to agonizing bodily pains. But the great desire he had of again joining his flock, made him forget his sufferings.

His longing was at last gratified, and the people of Magdeburg rejoiced greatly to have their beloved bishop among them once more. And they had reasons to be proud of him! Was he not the founder of a Religious Order, the Champion of the Eucharist, the great Reformer, and the Liberator of the Church? His name was celebrated throughout Europe. But these good people honored and loved him above all as a simple and humble religious, through whom God worked many miracles.

It was Holy Week, 1134, bringing with it the commemoration of Christ crucified. Making a superhuman effort to forget his pains, Norbert went to his cathedral church to perform the services of Holy Thursday. He wished to spend the entire night before the Blessed Sacrament, meditating on Our Saviour's agony in the garden, but his condition rendered this impossible; and, utterly exhausted, he returned to his house.

Supported only by the grace of God, and the energy of a strong will, he rose from his bed of pain to celebrate the Holy Sacrifice on Easter Sunday. It was the last Mass offered by St. Norbert.

From that time on he grew steadily worse. Realizing that the cold hand of death would soon take him from among his brethren, he summoned them to his bedside for his last instructions. He urged them to practice above all the virtues of faith and patience, which two he had cherished throughout life. "When striking with steel," he said "sparks of fire come forth. So also, by striking a heart of stone with lively faith, you can produce sparks of divine love.—Do you suffer persecution? Be patient. Are you better than your master?"

Part One: St. Norbert

Thus he continued to exhort them, while his countenance shone forth with tranquil joy and holy peace.

The Saint's illness became more serious. Finally, Norbert asked to receive the last Sacraments. Bishop Anselm administered the sacred rites and from then on remained almost constantly at his bedside. Norbert received the Body of Our Lord with extraordinary fervor and piety. With the Sacred Unction there had been a more copious infusion of the Holy Spirit into his soul; and, once more, he lovingly addressed his disciples. This was Pentecost, the third of June, 1134.

The Saint lingered until Wednesday, when finally, in full possession of his senses, he gave his last blessing to the Archdiocese and his Order, and then, invoking the Holy Names, he peacefully expired casting, a glance of angelic sweetness towards Heaven. Thus died Norbert, a humble missionary and a great Saint.

The Emperor ordered that Norbert's body be interred in an abbey of his order, St. Mary's at Magdeburg. The tomb constructed our saint quickly became known for the many miracles which took place at his intercession. Norbert was canonized by Pope Gregory XIII in 1582.

The Protestant revolt, and a century later the outbreak of the Thirty Years War forced the translation of Norbert's body from Magdeburg, which then was in the hands of the Protestants, to the Abbey of Strahov in Prague. Yet Norbert was not finished working miracles, as during the octave of his translation, six hundred Protestants abjured their errors and were restored to the unity of the Church. As a result, St. Norbert was declared the Patron of Bohemia.

The Death of St. Norbert

PART TWO
THE NORBERTINE ORDER

Chapter I
The Plans of St. Norbert

From the time of his ordination Norbert had cherished the idea of founding a religious order in the Church.

The true Christian life of self-denial, fervor and piety had well-nigh become extinct in many parts of Europe. To resuscitate this life and restore it to its primitive piety and splendor, he considered his divine mission.

Alone, he was powerless to stem the torrent of evil, and his attempts were bound to suffer shipwreck, had he not found disciples animated by the same spirit and willing to help and support him in his work.

We have narrated in the first part of this booklet how the Saint came in touch with the bishop of Laon and finally succeeded in accomplishing his plans.

A little information concerning the nature and history of this Order which he founded will not be unwelcome to the reader.

Chapter II
The Ends of the Order

The five particular ends of the Norbertine Order are prayer, zeal for the salvation of souls, the spirit of habitual penance, devotion to the Blessed Sacrament, and to our Lady.

These special ends of the Order are vividly illustrated in the life of St. Norbert. The two first arise from the nature of a canonical order, an order of priests. The third is taken from the monastic orders, the fourth and fifth are characteristics of St. Norbert's life and the Order which he founded.

Chapter III
Prayer

ST. Peter said, on the election of the first deacons. "*Nos vero orationi instantes erimus.*" "We will give ourselves continually to prayer."

The people were ignorant in religious matters, and many of their leaders were animated by a spirit of worldliness. Moreover, the baneful influences of secular interference in the spiritual activity of the clergy, was paralyzing the energies and impairing the vitality of Christianity.

Enthusiastically Norbert took upon himself the arduous task of reformation. He met with opposition on all sides, and soon realized how difficult it is to change old customs and inveterate abuses.

The Order of St. Norbert is an order of priests. The first duty of the priest is to offer sacrifice and to pray. St. Norbert's idea was to revive the apostolic spirit among the clergy; and great apostles are always preeminently men of prayer. The Sacrifice of the Mass and the devout recitation of the Divine Office are the most perfect expression of religious worship.

The Divine Office was sadly neglected in the time of St. Norbert but, as we read in the preface of our Constitutions: "God, Whose nature is goodness, Whose will is power, Whose works are mercy, wishing to resuscitate in His Church the apostolic spirit, then well-nigh extinguished, had prepared by His grace St. Norbert to do this work."

"As a fish cannot live out of the water," Norbert used to say, "so a man cannot live without prayer." Prayer is the great law of human life.

"If you would suffer the trials and sorrows of this life patiently, be a man of prayer.

"If you would know the devices of Satan and would foil his deceits, be a man of prayer.

"If you would live in joy and walk sweetly in the path of penance, be a man of prayer.

"If you would nourish your soul with the marrow of devotion and would always have it filled with good thoughts and good desires, be a man of prayer.

"If you would strengthen and confirm your courage in the ways of God, be a man of prayer. It is through prayer that we receive the union and grace of the Holy Spirit, who teaches all things.

"Further, if you would mount to the heights of contemplation and enjoy the sweet embraces of the Bridegroom, exercise yourself in prayer."

This magnificent eulogy of prayer, written by a medieval mystic, expresses aptly the sentiments of Norbert and his disciples.

Chapter IV
Zeal For Souls

Zeal for the salvation of souls is an act of intense charity whereby we seek ardently the glory of God and the spiritual welfare of our neighbor. This care of souls is the second end of the Canons Regular of St. Norbert.

It arises from the nature of the Order, which is partly contemplative and partly active.

Like the Apostles, the Norbertines are bound to give themselves continually to prayer and the ministry of the Word. Cornelius a Lapide remarks: "It was the office of the Apostles to pray for themselves and for the whole Church; in prayer they received from God what they were to teach and to preach."

"Our Order," says the preface of the Norbertine Statutes, "is the propagation of God's glory; it is zeal for souls; the administration of the Sacraments; service in the Church of God. Our Order is to preach the Gospel, to teach the ignorant, to have the direction of souls, to perform pastoral duties."

In the age of St. Norbert, these priestly duties were sadly neglected. The clergy were not numerous; often ill prepared for their ministry, and their manner of life was often lax and licentious. There were, indeed, noble exceptions of zealous bishops and priests; but much had to be done to put the ecclesiastical organization in good order.

We all admire the courage, fortitude and prudence, displayed by that noble champion of justice and liberty, the great Pope Gregory VII. He fought successfully the laxity and licentiousness of the times and checked the unscrupulous encroachments attempted by civil rulers on the rights of the Holy See. But zealous bishops, learned and pious priests, fervent and devoted missionaries had yet to be formed. What the age needed most were homes of piety and learning, training-schools for the clergy; and this need was supplied by the Norbertine Order.

St. Norbert was the Charles Borromeo of the twelfth century; and the Norbertine abbeys were the seminaries of zealous missionaries, priests and bishops.

Chapter V
The Spirit Of Penance

By word and example Norbert inculcated the spirit of perpetual penance, service and sacrifice.

Charles Hugo, the historian of the Order, writes: "As the penances which St. Norbert had embraced after his conversion were greater than those which the mild rule of the canons exacted, he added to his Order the austerities of monastic institutes, so that it might not be wanting in anything that would contribute to the perfection of its members."

This spirit of penance was explained by St. Norbert to his disciples in the famous discourse which he addressed to them before leaving Prémontré. "Having of your own free will and from pure love of God renounced your earthly possessions, and even your own selves, you are daily obliged to carry the cross of Christ; that is, you are obliged to mortify continually your passions and to spend your whole life in works of penance."

In his "*Monita Spiritualia*" we read: "Those who understand how to appreciate penance, find therein an abundance of delight. A life of austerities bears a rich crop of happiness, but no one believes it unless he has experienced it."

The Norbertine life, consequently, combines the duties of priests with the mortifications of monks.

Besides fasting and abstinence, there are many ways of doing penance. To bear and to forbear, to conquer one's self, to observe accurately the rules of community life, frequently constitute the most difficult acts of penance.

Chapter VI
Devotion To The Blessed Sacrament

Eucharistic worship constitutes the fourth end of the Norbertine Order. In pictures, engravings, and statues, St. Norbert is often represented as holding in his hand a monstrance, while the heretic Tankelin lies prostrate at his feet.

The monstrance is the emblem of his devotion to the Holy Eucharist, and the prostrate Tankelin symbolizes Norbert's glorious triumph over the sacramentarian errors of this fanatical foe of the Mass and the Real Presence.

As God chose St. Peter to conquer Simon Magus, and opposed Athanasius to Arius, Cyril to Nestorius, Jerome to Jovinian, and Augustine to the Manicheans, so He selected St. Norbert as His champion when the heretic Tankelin stretched forth his impure hands to profane the Eucharist.

St. Norbert bequeathed devotion to the Blessed Sacrament as a special legacy to his sons. The pictures and statues that represent him with the monstrance in his hand seem to say: "Love the Eucharist. Defend and promote devotion to the Sacrament of the Altar! 'My children, forget not my law and let your hearts keep my commandments; for they shall add to your length of days and years of life and peace.'"[1]

Norbert inculcated in the minds of his disciples, cleanliness about the altar and fervor in the celebration of the Divine Mysteries. "At the altar," he used to say, "one shows his faith and love of God"; and again, "Bees fly from flower to flower to gather honey, so must a soul, to obtain devotion, dwell in meditation on the various mysteries of faith, especially before the Blessed Sacrament and in Holy Communion."

He exhorts his sons to: "meditate frequently on God Incarnate in the stable, on the Spouse of fair love, who at the Last

---

[1] Proverbs III: 1-2.

Supper gave His Own Flesh and Blood, and on the Lamb slain on Calvary. From these three furnaces you can draw forth burning fire to quicken your faith and enkindle your charity."

From the furnace of the Tabernacle he drew forth the burning flame that enlightened his extraordinary faith and enkindled his love for God and souls. In the midst of his trials and troubles he would spend hours in prayer and meditation before the altar; and, before any important undertaking, he would offer devoutly the Holy Sacrifice of the Mass to obtain light from Heaven.

The Holy Eucharist is the visible center of the Catholic religion. It is the greatest gift of God to man. Theologians call it the mirror of God's wisdom, the abridgment of all His wonders, the fountain of grace, the magnet of souls. It is the antidote for our daily sins, the food of angels, the bread of the strong. The other sacraments give to, or increase in the soul the life of Christ; the Eucharist is Christ.

In this school the Norbertine must learn his daily duties and pray for strength to execute them faithfully and conscientiously. The Holy Eucharist must be to him all in all.

In the tabernacle Christ practices the hidden and contemplative life. There He sings the most sublime canticle of praise to His Eternal Father. There He teaches the highest art and most sublime science of devout, reverent and affective prayer.

The Holy Eucharist also animates the priest with true zeal for the salvation of souls. From the tabernacle Jesus says: "My son, give me thy heart." The priest, while praying before the altar and listening to the tender pleadings of the God of mercy and compassion, learns how to draw the cold and indifferent hearts of men to the living Heart of the Savior.

The Holy Eucharist teaches eloquently the spirit of penance, service and sacrifice. Our Sacramental Savior is not loved as much as He deserves or ought to be loved —nay, often He is treated with carelessness, coldness, and contempt; sometimes even He is outraged. The priest who loves the Eucharist, prays, weeps and does penance for his own sins and the sins of the world, and thus he consoles and comforts his outraged Lord in the tabernacle.

The Order of St. Norbert has a special feast to commemorate its Founder's love and devotion to the Sacrament of the Altar. St. Norbert's glorious triumph over the deadly heresy of Tankelin is celebrated on the day after the feast of the Sacred Heart of Jesus.

Several confraternities have been canonically erected under the invocation of St. Norbert, to promote devotion to the Holy Eucharist among the faithful,—e.g., the Confraternity of the Blessed Sacrament and St. Norbert, and the Arch-confraternity of the Holy Mass of Reparation.

Chapter VII
Devotion To Our Lady

norbert said: "He is not a true son of the Virgin Mother of God, who is not with his whole heart devoted to her." These words express the spirit of Norbert's devotion to our Lady.

The preface to the Statutes of the Order tells us: "His disciples should be filled with the same spirit; Norbert wished them to honor and venerate in a most devout manner, the Blessed Virgin Mary, the most Holy Mother of God, the Patroness of the whole Order."

Indeed, the Blessed Virgin is, in a special manner, the Protectress of the Norbertine Order. From its foundation she has watched over it with a mother's tenderness and solicitude. Whilst Norbert was praying fervently in the chapel of St, John the Baptist, in the valley of Prémontré, that God might direct him in founding his Order, the Queen of Heaven appeared to him and told him that his prayers were heard. She indicated the place where he was to build the first church of the Order, and gave him the white habit saying: "Receive, my son, this white habit." Finally, she inspired him to ask the Sovereign Pontiff to confirm his Order.

The Roman Martyrology commemorates this apparition on the 5th of August. "*Eodem die apparitio ejusdem Beatissimae Virginis quae Sancto Patri Norberto canonicum instituti habitum in capella Sancti Joannis Baptistae*

Praemonstrati ostendit." (On the same day the apparition of the Blessed Virgin, who in the chapel of St. John the Baptist at Prémontré showed Saint Norbert the white habit of the Order.)

Devotion to the Immaculate Conception in particular is a distinctive mark of the Norbertines. Saint Norbert himself composed an office in honor of Mary Immaculate, from which I quote this sentence: "I hail thee, O Virgin, who by the preservation of the Holy Ghost hast triumphed over the formidable sin of our first parents, without being tainted by it."

In the *Monita Spiritualia* or Spiritual Counsels, which contain extracts from the writings of the Saint, we read as follows: "The intention of the Mother of fair love in adorning us with the white habit—a symbol of purity—was none other than to teach us a true devotion to her Immaculate Conception. Wherefore, if your heart is not inflamed with love; if you do not possess virginal chastity, you are a member of the Order only in name and dress."

One of the Conventual Masses, called *De Beata*, is said daily in each abbey in honor of Our Lady. The vigils of all the principal feasts of the Blessed Virgin are days of fast and abstinence. A great number of churches belonging to the Order are dedicated to the Ever-Blessed Mother of God.

There have, at all times, been numerous members of the Order whose holy lives were remarkable for their tender devotion to Our Lady.

Blessed Adam, afterwards bishop of Whithorn in Scotland, a well-known ascetical and mystical theologian of the twelfth century, writes: "Mary is our mistress, our advocate, our sweetness and our life, our hope and our mediatrix. She is the Mother of God, the Queen of Angels, the conqueror of devils, the refuge of the sorrowful, the solace of the orphans, the strength of the weak, the support of the just."

One of the sweetest medieval poets is Blessed Herman of Cologne. He was the first singer who composed a hymn in honor of the Sacred Heart; and he has written many songs in honor of Mary, to whom he was mystically espoused, and was, consequently, called by the name of Joseph.

Chapter VIII
SS. Norbert And Augustine

The place for the cradle of the Norbertine Order had been pointed out by Divine Providence.

That same night, during which St. Norbert prayed in the chapel of St. John the Baptist, our Lady appeared to him and gave him the white habit.

But when disciples began to gather about Norbert, they needed a rule of life. Some suggested the Carthusian, others the Benedictine rule. Neither of these corresponded to the ideals of the Founder. He was an apostle and he wished to train apostles, not hermits or monks. He was a penitent and he looked for souls willing to do penance and to sacrifice their own will and judgment. How to combine the apostolic and the penitential life? "Pray," he said to his sons, "pray fervently that God may manifest to us His holy will. He alone can enlighten us in this difficult matter."

On his missionary journeys St. Norbert had often realized the crying need of holy and learned priests. He wished his disciples to be teachers and preachers, to teach all nations and to preach the Gospel to every creature.

After long and devout meditation his prayers were heard.

One of the brethren had been thinking seriously which rule should be adopted. One day, not because of his own merits, but owing to the fervent prayers of his brethren, Saint Augustine appeared to him. Having in his right hand his own rule, he said: "I am Augustine, Bishop of Hippo. Behold the rule I have written. If your brethren, who are my sons, fight bravely under this standard, they will stand without fear before God's judgment seat."

Norbert himself was the fortunate brother favored with this celestial vision. Out of humility he refused to divulge his name.

APPARITION OF ST. AUGUSTINE
Engraved by Theodore Gallus (1622)

Chapter IX
The Norbertine Canons

FROM the earliest age of Christianity there were priests who lived in communities, followed a rule (canon), and possessed all things in common. Differing from the monks, they were priests, living around the bishop and attached to a cathedral or collegiate church. In this church and elsewhere they conducted religious services and some of them taught in cathedral or abbey schools.

The canons regular did not differ from the secular clergy in religious and ecclesiastical activity; they differed in this, that they added the monastic life to that of their priestly vocation.

Such an order of Canons or priests was founded by St. Norbert after he had failed in reforming the secular canons of Xanten and Laon.

The Order of St. Norbert has adapted itself to all times and conditions. "Ready for every good work" is its motto. We see the Norbertines over more than eight centuries as educators and pastors, as preachers and confessors, as writers and missionaries.

Though Norbert had principally in mind the formation of a saintly and learned clergy, he also admitted lay Brothers to serve the priests in the temporal affairs of the community by the performance of manual labor. They wear a white or grey habit and are not obliged to the recitation of the Divine Office.

Chapter X
The Norbertine Sisters

A similar division of choir and lay-Sisters is found in the convents of Norbertine canonesses, a second order for women founded by St. Norbert.

Apostolic men in the early Middle Ages did not think it proper to deprive women of the blessings of the religious life. Hence St. Norbert, after founding a home for the training of priests, also made provisions for a convent of Sisters.

The first woman who placed herself under Norbert's spiritual direction was a noble lady of Vermandois, the widow of

Raymond of Clastres. She is known in history as Blessed Ricvera. Having given part of her property for the sustenance of Norbert's brethren, she lived herself in the neighborhood of the abbey in a poor little but and devoted her time and talents to the care of the sick.

In due time Norbert gave her the white habit and the veil. Thus the little cottage became the cradle of the Second Order of St. Norbert, which has flourished for centuries and exists to this day in various countries.

Chapter XI
The Third Order

HAVING founded an Order for priests and Sisters who dwell within the sacred precincts of the monastery, Norbert asked himself whether it would not be possible to open the doors of his institute to persons living in the world.

One of the most famous converts of St. Norbert was Count Godfrey of Cappenberg. Many Christians admired the sudden change by which a proud prince was transformed into a humble religious, and a riotous court into a peaceful monastery. This example appealed with special force to the French nobleman, Count Theobald.

This illustrious personage was the most powerful prince in the kingdom of France. He was the first in rank after the king himself. He had as father, Stephen, count of Champagne and Blois; and, as mother, Alice, daughter of William the Conqueror.

Theobald was an ideal Christian prince, who had no other object than to secure the happiness of his people and to encourage them in the practice of virtue.

One day he came to Norbert to obtain his advice. As the Bollandists tell us, "he was so charmed by the eloquence of the man of God, the sweetness of his countenance and the wisdom of his answers, that he offered himself entirely to St. Norbert with all his possessions."

Norbert knew that Theobald was the father of the orphans, the defender of widows, and the supporter of the poor. He told him it was the will of God that he should remain in the world and there edify the people by the beauty of a virtuous,

Christian life. Before sending him away, however, he drew up for him a rule of life containing special practices easy of observance in the world and sufficiently strict to become for souls of good will, a protection against the evils of the age and a safe road to heaven.

"It was the first institution of its kind and was imitated in subsequent years by several other founders, notably St. Francis and St. Dominic." Thus writes Father Durand in his "*Manuel des Ordres Religieux.*"

By the creation of a third order, Norbert introduced the religious life into the bosom of the family and the whirl of secular pursuits.

Chapter XII
Decline Of The Order

IN the early days of its existence the Order grew rapidly. In 1230, the Norbertines counted twenty-nine provinces, with six hundred and sixty three abbeys.

Part TWO: The Norbertine Order

Many of these abbeys were richly endowed; and the wealth itself was a cause of decay. The religious revolt of the sixteenth century dealt a heavy blow to the Order. Most of its houses were situated in Northern Europe, where the "Great Pillage" took place. As they grew in property they did not increase in sanctity; besides, the growth in riches brought about the envy of evil-minded aristocrats who robbed the Church to enrich themselves. The houses in Germany, Scandinavia, Holland, England, Scotland and Ireland were destroyed or confiscated by rapacious "reformers." The abbeys and priories, in Austria, France, and Belgium continued to flourish until the imperial sexton, Joseph II, and the French Revolution destroyed almost every vestige of the order.[2]

---

[2] Joseph II (1741-1790), was the Austrian Emperor who embraced "Febronianism", a heresy holding that the state was the guarantor of the rights of the Church and attempted to form a national Church along those lines. The French Revolution embodied similar thinking with the constitution of the clergy. Consequently the Order was expelled.

Chapter XIII
The Revival

The last hundred years have witnessed a marvelous rebirth of the Order. In the words of Pope Benedict XV, "To see this same Order, as it were, rising from its ruins, repairing the losses it has suffered, and once again spreading throughout those very localities where it had been suppressed and rooted out, is, indeed, a source of astonishment. Hence, we rejoice to observe how the members of the Premonstratensian Order are persistently laboring in all those works which tend to promote the glory of God, and the salvation of souls. It is especially pleasing to Us to recognize in you the same spirit bequeathed to you by your holy Founder and Lawgiver; We mean the spirit of an active love towards the August Sacrament, of filial devotion to the Immaculate Mother of God, and of faithful attachment to this Apostolic See."

Revived in Europe, the Order has spread to Asia, Africa, North and South America. One of the most flourishing abbeys is located in the United States.

Chapter XIV
A Prospect

THE first church of the Order was built at Prémontré, France. Its consecration took place in 1122. A large multitude of people had gathered from all directions to assist at the solemn ceremonies. Through the midst of the numerous bystanders the sacrificial stone was carried to the sanctuary. It fell and was broken to pieces, so that the consecration ceremonies had to be repeated.

St. Norbert saw in the event a prophecy. He foretold that in the course of centuries his Order would be broken to pieces but would be restored. Indeed the Norbertines were scattered, exiled and killed, and the Order broken to pieces by the Protestant Reformation and the French Revolution, but it has been restored; and the sons of St. Norbert gird themselves once again, after the example of their Founder, to fight the battles of the Church and to win the world for Christ.

St. Norbert and His Order

As Pope Pius IX wrote, "An Order which has done so much good for the Church will never perish."

PART THREE
NORBERTINE SAINTS

The Order of St. Norbert has produced a large number of men and women eminent for piety and virtue. History records the names of several Norbertines, confessors, martyrs, and virgins, who are honored as Saints of Holy Church. The "*Hagiologium Norbertinum*" gives a Saint for almost each day of the year, with a short account of their lives.

Saint Evermode

Evermode was one of the first disciples of St. Norbert. Touched by his sermons at Cambray, he asked leave to become one of St. Norbert's followers. The purity of his life and his zeal for the glory of God endeared him to St. Norbert. Never was novice more fervent, never priest more zealous. He was Norbert's beloved disciple, his joy and consolation, so much so that the Saint wished to have Evermode always near him. He chose him as one of his companions on his missionary journey to Antwerp to labor for the conversion of the people seduced by

Tankelin. He took him to Cologne to obtain relics for his new church; to Rome for the confirmation of his Order and when in 1126, St. Norbert became Archbishop of Magdeburg, he once more asked Evermode to go with him. He was made the superior of the first Norbertine foundation in that city. Here he shared St. Norbert's sufferings, toils, and victories and when the holy Founder was at last on his bed of suffering, St. Evermode was constantly near his beloved father, whose salutary exhortations he received with the most profound reverence, and whose last counsels he stored in his own heart. After the death of St. Norbert, Evermode buried the body of his beloved master and became its faithful guardian.

In the year 1159, Evermode was elected bishop of Ratzberg, near Bremen. The diocese of Ratzberg had been established in 1062. Aristo was its first bishop. After the death of Aristo, a persecution arose and the See was left vacant for more than eighty years. During this time the country, never fully Christianized, relapsed into paganism.

Here was a large field for Evermode's fiery but prudent zeal.

To work more successfully, he established a monastery of Norbertine canons in the episcopal city. The zealous efforts of the priests were crowned with success. Apostate Catholics returned to the fold, and pagans received the light of faith. Evermode travelled from place to place, instructing the people and organizing the diocese. He is truly called the apostle of the Wends, a people of Slavic origin, who dwelt near the coast of the Baltic Sea. He defended the liberties of the Church against secular princes who claimed the right of investiture. Full of days and good works, he went to his eternal reward on February 17, in the year of our Lord, 1177. His feast is kept on the same day.

Saint Isfrid

After the death of St. Evermode, the canons of the cathedral gathered for the election of a new bishop. Their choice fell upon Saint Isfrid, superior of the Norbertine monastery of Jerichow, in the diocese of Havelberg.

Isfrid was a man of extensive learning, solid piety, and of an austere life. The chronicles of the diocese call him: "sanctus sancti successor"—a saint succeeding a saint. Like his predecessor, Isfrid went from place to place, preaching the word of God and administering the Sacraments. Through his gentleness and charity he soon gained the hearts of his people and gradually weaned them from their pagan customs and superstitions. He found a willing supporter in Henry, duke of Saxony, who had extended his dominions up to the Baltic Sea and who realized that Christianity was the best means of consolidating his new possessions.

But great sufferings were in store for Isfrid. Frederick Barbarossa, emperor of Germany, had deprived the duke of Saxony of his duchy, and had given it to Bernard, count of Anhalt. This impious prince persecuted all who did not approve of the emperor's policy against the pope and the Church. These persecutions, which Isfrid bore with dignity and patience, lasted until the duke of Saxony was reconciled to the emperor and regained his territory.

When, in the year 1195, the cathedral chapter of Schwerin, composed of Wend and Saxon canons, did not agree as to the election of a bishop, Isfrid was requested by the pope to act as arbitrator between the two parties. Brunward, belonging to the race of the Wends, was made bishop.

In spite of his arduous labors among the Wends and Saxons, Isfrid never relaxed his severe mode of life. How pleasing his austerities and prayers were to God is proved by the miracles which he worked during his life. When, on Good Friday, Isfrid, as usual, was fasting on bread and water, the water was miraculously changed to wine. One day when the bishop and his clergy were going in procession around the church, a blind man approached the bishop, beseeching him to restore his sight. Isfrid's tender heart was touched. He sprinkled the blind man with holy water, saying: "*Dominus illuminat caecos.*" (The Lord enlightens the blind.) At these words the blind man recovered the use of his eyes.

A Saint before God and man, Isfrid died on the 15th of June, 1204, an octogenarian. On that day his feast is celebrated.

Saint Ludolf

Another Saint, named Ludolph, ruled over the diocese of Ratzberg. In the monastery, St. Ludolf had always been noted for his strict observance of the rules and for his zeal and piety. After his election as bishop, he did not change his manner of living. On the contrary, knowing the needs of his diocese, he redoubled his vigils and prayers to draw God's blessings upon his labors. The various tribes which inhabited chiefly the northern parts of his diocese had, through the unwearied exertions of his predecessors, been brought into the fold of Christ; but there always remained the possibility of their being led astray by evil examples and the corrupted morals of neighboring tribesmen. Hence, burning with zeal for their salvation, Ludolf did not rest until he saw the laws of God and the Church conscientiously observed throughout the diocese. All access to error and corruption from without was warded off by his zeal and watchfulness. Unweariedly he labored among the people, instructing the ignorant, and consoling the sorrowful. All looked upon him as their beloved father and trusted protector.

Ludolf had a long conflict with Albert, duke of Saxony, regarding the rights and liberties of the Church. To such an extent did the duke pursue his evil designs that he wished to raze the cathedral and monastery, both situated near his castle, and to transform the place into a garden. To these proposals Ludolf would not listen. Nor could he be induced by promises or threats to give up what had been consecrated to God's service.

The duke then ordered some of his courtiers and soldiers to lay their hands on the bishop and throw him into a dark, dirty dungeon, and to detain him there until his consent should be extorted. It is impossible to describe the dreadful sufferings the saintly bishop had to endure at the hands of his impious jailors, but neither hunger nor thirst, nor tortures of any kind, could bend or break the bishop's constancy.

When the duke saw that the bishop was sinking under his severe sufferings, he became afraid of the clamors of the people, and therefore he sent Ludolf to the prince of Mecklenburg, at Weimar. But the bishop was so exhausted that he died from the effects of his prolonged agony, at Weimar, on March 29, in the year 1250. He is honored as a martyr for upholding the rights and liberties of the Church.

Saint Gilbert

Saint Gilbert, a rich nobleman of Auvergne, in France, was a crusader who, at the voice of St. Bernard, went forth with Louis VII, king of France.

Before going to the East, he requested his devoted wife, Petronella to guard their only daughter, Pontia, against all evils; and he charged her to be more generous in almsgiving during his absence, than was her wont.

On his return from the crusade, which had been a complete failure, Gilbert, his wife and daughter, formed the resolution to consecrate themselves to the service of God and the poor. Gilbert built a hospital for the sick, and also a convent for Norbertine nuns at Aubeterre, where Petronella and Pontia received the religious habit.

As for himself, he wished to lead the life of a hermit and retired to a lonely place called Neuffons or "Nine Fountains," but soon afterwards he went to the Norbertine abbey of Dilo, where he put himself under the direction of Abbot Onifrius.

Having made his profession he was sent to found the abbey of Neuffons. Of this abbey he became the first superior, so manifest were his merits and holiness.

Here he also built a hospital. Through humility and a spirit of mortification, he visited the sick, dressed and kissed their wounds, and frequently through God's grace, restored these sufferers to health and vigor.

Mothers used to bring their delicate and deformed children to Gilbert, who blessed them, reading over them the Gospel: "Suffer little children to come unto me, for theirs is the Kingdom of Heaven." To this day, Gilbert is invoked for the cure of sickly children.

Such was his love for the poor that he desired to be buried in the cemetery of the poor. He died on June 6, in the year 1152. His feast is celebrated on the 29th of October, the day of the translation of his relics.

Saint Frederick

St. Frederick was born at Hallum, in Friesland. He received his early education in his native town and completed his studies at Muenster, in Germany, where a flourishing school existed.

Truly devoted from infancy to the Mother of God, he put his chastity under her maternal protection. To St. John the Evangelist and to St. Cecily, his favorite patron saints, he daily commended the purity of his soul and body.

When, at the end of his classical course, he was deliberating and praying to know the state of life he should embrace, the Virgin Martyr, St. Cecily, appeared to him and told him that it was God's will that he should work, not only for his own salvation, but also for that of others.

Part Three: Norbertine Saints

Soon after, he returned to Hallum, where he taught Latin and likewise instructed the children in the Catholic doctrine.

Finally he was ordained priest and while teaching at the college, he assisted the aged parish priest in the discharge of his pastoral duties.

At the pastor's death, Frederick was chosen his successor and proved himself a model shepherd of Christ's flock, instructing the people, administering the sacraments, visiting the sick, helping the poor and spending much of his time in devout and fervent prayer.

Each Saturday he offered Mass in honor of the Blessed Virgin, through whose intercession he obtained many favors.

On one occasion he saw in a vision the impiety and iniquity of the world. He heard the voice of our Lady who appeared to him and said: "Flee out of Babylon!"

Feeling that he was called to a higher life, he obtained consent of his ordinary, the bishop of Utrecht, to join the Norbertines at the abbey of Mariengaard.

After having made his profession, he returned to Hallum to found there an abbey of the Order, which he named in honor of Mary, "Mariengaard," or "Mary's Garden." This happened in 1168. To this abbey he added a school for the education of Catholic youth.

Under his gentle, pious and prudent administration, a great number of postulants applied for admission into the Order.

He founded several other abbeys for priests and Sisters.

Having fallen ill, and feeling that his end was near, he said his last Mass, which he offered in honor of Mary, to thank his divine protectress for all the graces and favors received through her gracious and powerful intercession.

He died in 1175, on March 3. His grave became glorious and famous on account of numerous miracles. At the time of the Protestant Reformation his remains were removed to the Norbertine Abbey of Bonne-Esperance, in Belgium. This abbey, confiscated during the French Revolution, is at present the diocesan seminary of Tournay.

The feast of St. Frederick is kept on the third of March.

Saint Siard

In the college connected with the abbey of Mariengaard many of the most promising youths of Friesland received their elementary and classical education.

Among the many learned and holy men who were graduated from this school, there are two who have received the honors of the altar, viz., St. Siard and Blessed Herman Joseph.

St. Siard was born of noble parents in Friesland. Nature had endowed him with a clear and penetrating mind, a tender and devout heart, and other good qualities, which were perfected by faithful cooperation with God's grace.

Siard was still very young when he became a student at Mariengaard. In the course of time he was admitted into the Order, of which he became a most distinguished member.

At the death of Abbot John, Siard was elected to succeed him, becoming thus the fifth abbot of Mariengaard. His biographer remarks, "As the mantle of Elias had fallen on Eliseus, so the mantle of St. Frederick had fallen on Siard." The founder's double spirit of the contemplative and active life likewise rested on his saintly successor.

St. Siard, abbot of a large community, understood the words of the wise man: "Have they made thee ruler? Be not lifted up, be among them as one of them." He was an example of humility, sharing with his brethren the lowest and humblest labors of the community. The saints are just and gentle, and so was Siard. Though severe in maintaining true discipline, never would he let an angry word pass his lips.

He is frequently represented with a basket full of loaves, to indicate his generous kindness towards God's poor.

St. Siard died in 1230, November 13th. His body was first buried in the sacristy of the abbey church, but was afterwards transferred to a marble tomb near the choir stalls of the canons.

His successor, Sibrandus, who wrote his life, testifies to many miracles wrought at his tomb.

At the time of the Protestant Reformation, when impious men were wont to profane the most sacred objects, his relics were removed to a safer place in Germany. Later, they were divided between the abbey of St. Foillan in Hainault and the abbey of Tongerloo, near Antwerp. His feast is celebrated on the 17th of November.

Saint Godfrey

Godfrey (God's Peace), count of Cappenberg, in Westphalia, was the chief of one of the most illustrious families in the German empire. He was a descendant of Charlemagne and the Saxon Witikind while Jutta, his wife, was the daughter of the count of Arnsberg. High was his rank in the eyes of the world, but he attained a far higher nobility through his pure and virtuous life.

His Life, edited by the learned Bollandus, describes him "the meekest and gentlest of all the nobles: eloquent in discourse, prudent in counsel, brave in battle."

Having a tender and delicate conscience, he soon conceived a profound disgust for the world, and yearned to live for God alone.

In 1120, St. Norbert was preaching in Cologne. Godfrey had heard of Norbert, how, though Count Gennep and having a high position at the court of the Emperor, he had nevertheless left the service of all earthly rulers to devote his entire life to the service of God and souls.

Godfrey resolved to go to Cologne to listen to the famous preacher and to consult him concerning his own spiritual interests.

Deeply moved by the eloquence and piety of St. Norbert, Godfrey returned to Cappenberg, where he revealed his inmost thoughts and desires to his wife and younger brother Otto.

After mature deliberation the three resolved to change their castle into a religious house. Soon after, Godfrey and Otto received the white habit from the hands of St. Norbert, while Jutta took the veil in a convent of Norbertine nuns. They also founded two other abbeys, one at Ilbenstadt, in Hesse, and another at Varlar, near Coesfeld.

Such a change caused great consternation among the nobility, and Godfrey had to suffer ridicule, contempt and opposition from the Westphalian princes, especially from his father-in-law, the count of Arnsberg. Nothing, however, could divert him from the noble resolution he had bravely and generously formed.

St. Norbert built great hopes on him and wished to have so faithful and fervent a religious near him in the mother house. So Godfrey and his brother Otto went to Prémontré, where both received Holy Orders. This was in 1125.

In the following year, Norbert was elected archbishop of Magdeburg and he requested Godfrey to accompany him to his See. Soon after, Godfrey's health failed, and he was permitted to return to the abbey of Ilbenstadt.

His illness made rapid progress. When he was dying he saw the angels and saints of God coming to meet his soul; and he said: "Behold the messengers of my God and Creator! Oh how welcome they are!"

This took place in 1127, on January 13, when St. Godfrey was only 30 years old.

His feast is kept on the 16th of January.

Saint Gerlac

St. Gerlac was born in the 12th century, of noble parents, at Houthem, in the Netherlands, called at present, Houthem St. Gerlac. He was an officer in the army of the German emperor.

He had led a life of dissipation and sin until the grace of God touched him at a tournament of nobles at Julich, where he hoped to carry off again the prize for military skill and bravery.

When all were assembled and the tournament was about to begin, a messenger brought him sad news of the sudden death of his beloved wife. This sorrowful message overwhelmed him with almost uncontrollable grief, but it conveyed at the same time a salutary lesson. It unveiled to him the vanities of the world.

Part Three: Norbertine Saints

Without a moment's delay he left his aristocratic associates and returned to Houthem. Having put his affairs in order, he took the pilgrim's staff, visited various shrines, repaired to Rome and threw himself at the feet of Pope Eugenius III. He made a general confession to the Holy Father and asked for a severe penance in expiation of his sinful life.

The pope ordered him to go to Jerusalem and there to serve the sick and the poor in the hospitals for a period of seven years. After this time of severe penance combined with works of charity, Gerlac returned to Rome where he gave an account of his activities to the Sovereign Pontiff Adrian IV, who was educated in one of the schools of the Order and, according to some historians, was a member of the Norbertine family.

By the pope's advice he returned to Houthem to lead a hermit's life. Not far from the castle in which he was born there stood a hollow oak tree of large dimensions in which he made his dwelling place, a little matting being his bed and a stone his pillow.

Under the white habit of St. Norbert, which he had received, he carried various instruments of penance. Each day he visited the tomb of St. Servatius at Maastricht, and each Saturday he made a pilgrimage to the shrine of our Lady at Aix-la-chapel.

His favorite pious prayer was: "Lord have mercy on me, a sinner." Like St. Benedict Labre, he had much to endure from ill-disposed people who misunderstood his penances and pilgrimages.

When he was at the point of death, his biographer narrates that St. Servatius appeared to him and gave him the consolations of our holy religion.

He died in 1171, on January 5th. His feast is kept on the 14th of January.

St. Adrian and St. James

St. Adrian Jansens of Hilvarenbeek, in Holland, and St. James Lacoupe of Audenarde, in Belgium, are two of the nineteen martyrs of Gorcum.

Though these valiant champions of the Faith received the crown of martyrdom at

Briel, they are usually called the Martyrs of Gorcum, because in this latter city most of these martyrs had been thrown into prison and suffered unspeakable torments for their religion, inflicted upon them by murderous tyrants, whom lying historians have called "defenders of liberty."

Adrian and James received the white habit of St. Norbert in the abbey of Middelburg, in Dutch Zeeland, which abbey is still in existence, although now it serves as the courthouse of the city.

At the time of their martyrdom, Adrian was pastor at Monster, near the mouth of the river Maas. James was his assistant. Adrian had always been an exemplary religious; but James unfortunately, soon after his ordination had been led astray by the "new religion" and had given great scandal. However, through the prayers of his brethren and the mercy of God, he soon repented, returned to his abbey, and, having done penance for his apostasy, he strove to repair the scandal by preaching zealously and writing books in defense of the Faith. Thus he strengthened the faith of

Christians and brought many stray sheep back to the Fold.

The zeal with which Adrian and James fought for the Faith of their fathers made them all the more odious to the godless "reformers," whose energies were bent on robbing people of their religion, and the Church of its property.

Both priests were made captives and were delivered into the power of the count of Lummen, the fanatical and ferocious chief of a band of men, hardly less cruel and impious than himself.

When they arrived at Briel they were thrown, together with other confessors of the Faith, into a dark and filthy dungeon.

They suffered hunger, thirst, cold and indescribable indignities. They were marched in procession, two by two, their necks bound together by ropes. They were struck with rods and scourges, burning candles were applied to their lips, nostrils and ears; and other infernal torments were inflicted upon them, so that, of the twenty-one, two renounced their faith, being unable to bear any longer the agonizing pains with which these cruel savages tortured them.

Adrian and James fearlessly professed their faith before the Council of the Revolutionaries—styled "reformers" by our lying historians—rejoicing that they were allowed to suffer with Christ.

The "crime" for which they were condemned and sentenced to death was their belief in the Real Presence and the Primacy of St. Peter.

The nineteen martyrs were hanged, July 9, in the year 1572. They were beatified by Clement IX and canonized by Pius IX.

Blessed Herman Joseph

Herman Joseph was born at Cologne, about the year 1150. He was from infancy a privileged child of Mary.

When Herman was but a little child he was often observed to steal away to a church near his house, to kneel there before a statue of our Lady with the Divine Child, where he prayed with such lively faith and intense fervor as if he saw the Blessed Mother of God listening and speaking to him. He often brought a flower or an apple to give as a present to the Infant Jesus in Mary's arms. One day, the legend says, our Lady bent down to her little visitor and held the Divine Child towards him. Jesus deigned to take the apple from the eager hand of Herman and thus began that wonderful familiarity that the saintly Norbertine enjoyed all his life with the Mother and her Child.

At the age of twelve years Herman offered himself to the community of Steinfeld. There he attended school till he was sent to Mariengaard in Friesland, to finish his classical studies under St. Frederick. A few years later he commenced his novitiate at Steinfeld.

Among his religious brethren Herman was noted for his angelic purity and piety. On account of his tender devotion to Our Lady he was given the name of Joseph. Herman's humility was pained by this title; but Mary consoled him, for she appeared to him, the Child Jesus resting in her arms, saying: "You shall carry my Child as he was carried by my spouse, Joseph; and, because you have received the same privilege, you shall bear the same name."

The chronicler lingers delightfully on the simplicity and humility of Herman. He writes: "Oh if you had heard how simple and lowly he was in his speech, how ready he was to blame himself and excuse others, truly you would have said that he who abused himself to all was worthy to be raised above all. He never took heed of the good in himself, but was ever the first to take notice of the good in others. If he happened to be present when he was praised, he knew how to turn it off dexterously, in jest. There was nothing in his appearance that could be found fault with, even by the greatest zealot, but sanctity shone out in everything about him."

Indeed, the unmistakable light of holiness did shine through the veils which his humility folded round it; for we are told that his gentle presence was felt, not only as an incentive to perfection but as a check on the slightest relaxation of religious discipline and though he never reproved anyone, still the novices of Steinfeld candidly owned that they dreaded being remiss or unpunctual in their duties when Father Herman was in the abbey.

Little did he dream that any one regarded him in the light of an unconscious censor, while he was only grieving over his own unworthiness.

Herman was endowed with more than ordinary mental gifts, as is attested by a number of writings, among which are an interpretation of the Canticle of Canticles, and a series of songs and devotional tracts.

He was the first poet who composed a hymn in honor of the Sacred Heart — the well known "Ad Cor Jesu Salutatio."

To his love for contemplation and teaching he joined a taste for artistic labor. Tradition ascribes to him the construction of a timepiece for the abbey which anticipated the wonderful clocks of the craftsmen in the later Middle Ages.

Favors, temporal and spiritual, multiplied around the religious life of Herman: but he was also marked with the seal of the elect: grievous sufferings of body and mind, making him a living victim of God's love.

He offered the Holy Sacrifice of the Mass with angelic devotion; and wonderful graces were granted him during its celebration.

Active in God's service to the end, he fell sick while he conducted the Holy Week services for the Cistercian Sisters at Hoven. He died on Thursday after Easter, in 1241, a great example of faith, purity and love, over ninety years of age.

His feast is celebrated on the 8th of May. He is venerated as the patron of youth.

Blessed Rosnata

Rosnata was born in the ancient castle of his ancestors, at Tepl, Bohemia, about the year 1160. His father, Sezima, was a descendant of the counts of Mielnic and his mother, Droboslava, belonged to the princely family of Czernin, from which St. Ludmilla and St. Wenceslaus were likewise descended.

His truly Christian mother had consecrated him from his birth to the Blessed Mother of God, who took him under her maternal protection. When he came into the world, he was, to all appearance, a still-born child; but, by Mary's intercession, he grew into a strong and healthy boy. He was miraculously preserved from death when the heavy wheels of a carriage passed over his tender limbs; and, again when he had fallen into a river.

Though young in years and rich in worldly possessions, Rosnata was endowed with all the virtues and the noble character of a Christian knight. His charity towards the poor was boundless. His spotless life, his prudent judgment, his sound mind, his impartiality in rendering justice, gained him the love and confidence of rich and poor.

He married a young lady belonging to one of the most distinguished families of the country. After years of expectation they rejoiced in the birth of a son; but their joy was of short duration, for the child died; and shortly after, the mother followed it to its heavenly home.

Bitter was the trial, but Rosnata saw in it the finger of God. He built near his castle a monastery in honor of Our Lady, and placed it in charge of the Norbertines of the abbey of Strahov, near Prague.

After his return from Palestine, whither he had gone to fight the Saracens, he established a convent for Norbertine Sisters in his castle of Choteschau, where three of his sisters took the veil.

Feeling that he himself was called to the religious life, he went to Rome to consult the Holy Father, who invested him with his own hand with the white habit of St. Norbert and ordained him subdeacon.

Having returned to his native country, he became a member of the community of Tepl, which abbey he had founded.

In the blessed solitude of the cloister he gave himself entirely to the service of God. During the last years of his life he had to suffer much from avaricious, envious aristocrats who had cast their greedy eyes on the property of the abbey. They waylaid him and carried him off to one of their castles where they tortured him to death. Thus he died the death of a martyr on the 14th of July, 1217.

His feast is kept on the 19th of July.

Blessed Hugh

The first successor of St. Norbert at Prémontré was Blessed Hugh of Fosse. He was chaplain and secretary to Bishop Burchard of Cambray, when he begged to be admitted as a disciple of St. Norbert. He was the first novice of the holy Founder, and for many years the constant companion of his journeys, labors and trials, until he finally succeeded Norbert as superior of the Motherhouse, as had been declared in a celestial vision.

The higher Hugh rose in dignity, the lower he descended in humility. He never signed his name as "Abbot," but as "servant of God and of Norbert." More than once a diocese was offered to him, but he persistently declined the episcopal dignity, wishing rather to be hidden and unknown in the world, and loving to be alone with God and his brethren in the monastery.

Hugh labored zealously for the spread of the Order, and lived to see it expand its branches from the North Sea to the Mediterranean.

Part Three: Norbertine Saints

"He was loved by men and hated by the devil," says the chronicler. To all men he showed himself kind, meek, and charitable, edifying them by his holy life, and guiding them by wise and prudent counsel.

Finally, by increasing toil and labors, by daily fastings and by vigils of prayer, his body became exhausted. After ruling the Order for more than thirty years with signal sanctity and eminent wisdom, he felt the end of his earthly pilgrimage approaching. Calling his brethren together, he exhorted them for the last time to mutual charity and the faithful observance of their religious and priestly duties.

Fervent devotion to the Eucharist was a characteristic virtue of Blessed Hugh. This virtue he had learned from his father Norbert. "The Holy Mass," he used to say, "is the sum of our salvation." With ardent love and edifying reverence, he received the Last Sacraments, and peacefully slept in the Lord.

After the death of Hugh there occurred many miracles which bore witness to his eminent sanctity. Many sick were cured by touching his relics; and when his body was exhumed fifty years after his death, his bones emitted a wonderfully fragrant odor, a symbol of his holy life.

His feast is celebrated on the tenth day of February.

Blessed Walter

Blessed Walter was one of the early disciples of St. Norbert. Kindness to the poor was a prominent trait of his childhood days. Whatever he did not need for personal use he distributed to the poor of Christ.

When he had been admitted at Prémontré as a disciple of St. Norbert he strove to outdo every one in humility, generosity, and punctual observance of the Rule, so that he became a model of all virtues, a perfect image of his revered Master Norbert.

Walter was elected abbot of St. Martin's Abbey at Laon, when this abbey was in great poverty, which he bore with exemplary patience and cheerfulness. When God blessed the abbey, Walter was so generous and hospitable that whatever was not needed for the brethren, he distributed among the unfortunate who begged his assistance.

Blessed Walter was very moderate and abstemious at the table, wore the hairshirt constantly, slept on the bare ground or on a board, and spent every other night in prayer.

When Bishop Bartholomew resigned his episcopal see, Walter was appointed in his stead; but though living out of the abbey, he strictly kept the Rule and constitutions, and maintained even in the episcopal palace the rigor of his former life. When he became infirm, and realized that death was imminent, he called his religious brethren and the poor to his bedside, and while they were praying, his soul returned to the Creator.

His body, acording to his wish, was buried at Prémontré.

His feast is celebrated on the sixth of June.

Saint Gertrude

St. Gertrude was the youngest child of Louis, the Landgrave of Hesse and Thuringia and of that sweet medieval saint, Elizabeth of Hungary.

She was born on the feast of St. Michael, the 29th of September, 1227, eighteen days after the death of her father, who had joined the Crusade and died in Apulia, on his way to the Holy Land.

St. Elizabeth had made a vow to consecrate the child to God — if a boy, in the Norbertine abbey of Rommersdorff; if a girl, in the Norbertine convent of Altenberg, near Marburg.

When the child was eighteen months old, her holy mother took her to Altenberg, which convent she visited frequently, remaining sometimes for a considerable time there, as if she were one of the community.

St. Elizabeth died on November 19, 1231. Her last prayer was: "Oh Mary, come to my assistance. The moment has come when God summons his friend to the wedding feast. The Bridegroom seeks his spouse." Shortly after her death she appeared to her daughter, who was then only four years old.

It is easily understood that a child of so holy a mother made rapid progress in religious perfection; nor is it surprising to learn that, at the death of Mother Christina, in 1248, Gertrude was elected to succed her as abbess of Altenberg.

Under her prudent and pious administration the community continually advanced in the spiritual life, as well as in material prosperity. She built the church and enlarged the convent buildings. In this church she exposed for veneration numerous relics from her holy mother. She also preserved her mother's nuptial ring, her bridal dress and some statues of the Blessed Virgin, which latter she placed in different parts of the convent, so that the Sisters might have always before their eyes the image of our Lady, the model of perfect religion.

Singularly devoted to the Blessed Sacrament, she organized Eucharistic processions in and near the convent.

In order to help the crusaders in their fight against the followers of Mohammed, she instituted, with the sanction of the Holy Father, a crusade of prayers and penances.

She died, the 13th of August, 1297, at the age of 70 years, all of which, with the exception of eighteen months, she had passed within the sacred walls of the convent. Her feast is kept on the 13th of August.

Saint Bronislava

Saint Bronislava was born in 1203, at Kamien, in Silesia. Her father's name was Stanislaus, count of Prandota-Odroway, and her mother was Anna, of the noble family of Jaxa-Okolski. St. Hyacinth and St. Ceslaus were her first cousins, both being sons of Eustace, her paternal uncle.

From her infancy, Bronislava had given her heart to God. At the age of sixteen she left the world, which she had scarcely known, to take the veil in the Norbertine convent of Zwierzyniec, near Cracow, on the banks of the Vistula. This was in 1219, the year that her cousin, St. Hyacinth, who is called "the Flower of the Dominican Order," founded the priory of the Holy Trinity, in Cracow.

In the cloister Bronislava was ever a model to her Sisters by her exact observance of monastic discipline. To the penances prescribed by the Rule she added others to mortify her senses, and to obtain perfect mastery over herself. In her great humility, she often threw herself at the feet of her Sisters, begging their prayers, and deeming herself unworthy to be their companion. Her detachment from the world was complete.

The crucifix was her book of meditation. Frequently she retired to a lonely spot near the convent, now called Mount St. Bronislava in order to meditate more devoutly and lovingly on the Passion of our Redeemer. There our Lord appeared to her, saying: "Bronislava, My cross is thy cross, but My crown will also be thy crown."

On the feast of our Lady's Assumption, St. Bronislava, while praying in the convent chapel, was consoled by another heavenly vision. She saw heaven opened and our

Lady, with hosts of angels, resting over the Dominican priory of Cracow, and thence returning to heaven with St. Hyacinth, who had just died.

Henceforth Bronislava belonged more to heaven than to earth. It pleased God to call this privileged spouse to the kingdom of eternal bliss on the 29th of August, 1259, two years after the death of her cousin, St. Hyacinth.

Her feast is celebrated on the 30th of August.

Made in the USA
Monee, IL
23 April 2021

66621487R00066